They call me mother. I call me crazy.

Cortnei-Jai Mccrae

BookLeaf Publishing

Presentation by *BookLeaf Publishing*

Web: www.bookleafpub.com

E-mail: info@bookleafpub.com

ISBN: 9789357214438

First edition 2023

DEDICATION

I dedicate this book to my beautiful daughters Ruby-Roze and Jessika.

ACKNOWLEDGEMENT

I would like to thank the following people, without whom I would not have been able to complete this book, they gave me the strength and courage to achieve my dreams and for that I thank you. My Headspace worker and all of the lovely people from Relationships Australia.

My Eldest Daughter

Eldest
Big sister
Caring, compassionate, kind
My reason for living
I love you
My strong
Girl

My Youngest Daughter

Youngest
Intelligent, beautiful, kind
My reason for living
I love you
My baby
Girl

Your Mother's Imbrace

Smuggling close in your warm imbrace
In your mothers arms is a safe place
You're never alone, so do not fear
Because your mother will always be here

Growing Older

10 little fingers
10 little toes
And a cute little baby noise
My darling daughters here in my arms
My love protects you from all harm
So grow big and grow strong
Go travel near and travel far
And always remember you're never alone
And you'll always be welcome here at home

I would do it all again

I've been through hell
I've been through harm
But I would go through it all again
Just to have yous in my arms
You are my world
You are my life
Because the day yous were born
Yous became my life

My 5 year olds (Ruby-Roze) mind

Mum is the cheeky monkey
I am the cheeky Elephant
and my sister is a cheeky unicorn
We are all different
but we are all the same
We are a family

Hush my baby

Hush little baby don't say a word
Mamas gonna buy you a Mockingbird
and if that mockingbird don't sing
then mamas gonna buy you a diamond ring And if
that diamond ring don't shine
Mama's going to bake you a yummy pie
And if that yummy pie is old
then you'll still be the sweetest little girl In the world

Mother

Maternal
Over thinker
Thoughtful
Hard worker
Energetic
Right

Every night with a baby

It's 3am and you won't stop crying
I hold you in my arms
And show you everything's OK
This is very tiring
Every night it's the same old thing
I rock you in my arms as I start to sing
It's very tiring being a mother
But this is my life I don't want another
Because eventhough it gets tough
There is no place I would rather be
Then sitting here at 3am with you beside me

My daughters

My little princess
my shining star
you are perfect
Just the way you are
You are my angel
my darling girl
You Make me happy
In this crazy world

My mother

You were ment to be there for me
But you just left me
To live in misery
I'm all grown now and have kids of my own
Unlike with you my house is a happy home
I love my kids
And their never alone
Cos this is not just a house it is my home

Butter

You
Better buy
A better brand
Of better butter
Before breakfast
Baby

Chicken Nugget Pants

What does that mean to me
It could be
Pants made out of chicken nuggets
Pants for chicken nuggets
How wired would that be to see
How about Pants that taste like chicken nuggets
Or chicken nuggets that taste like Pants
So now I ask you the question
What dose this mean to you.
Would you have a clue

My subconscious mind

Alown in the dark
I sit and wait
Unknown to the world
Our Unknown fait
Then something movies in the dark
It's creeping closer
I hold my breath because I don't want to see
That the thing in the dark is actually me
Because I'm my own worst enemy

Passed on

Once by my side
But now your gone
Always in my heart
And by my side
Even if I can't see you
RIP

Pets not forgotten, Magik, Sabrina, mew mew, morticy and rigby, Shelly and fish

Your memories live on
In my heart
Even though
We are a part
I love and miss you with all my heart

My ex husband

You put me through hell
it felt like I was locked in a cell
but then she changed my fate
and we finally got to escape
because my daughter was the key
that finally set us free
She gave me the strength to leave the cell
So together we escaped from the living hell
Now we are safe
And happiness has taken its place

My favourite pokemon

Brave
Useful
Loveable
Big-hearted
Adventurous
Strong
Affectionate
Unstoppable
Responsible

Midnight rain

Thunder rumbles low in the dead of night
It starts to rain
What a beautiful sight
Rain drops dancing on the ground
Shimmering in the full moon light
This is such a beautiful sight
On this full moon night

Our story

We each have a story to tell
in this crazy world
You will always find darkness in our lives
so you've got to strive to find the light
Because this book is not over
the chapter is not done.
Because we all get a chance to tell our story

How far I've come

I've come so far
From the little I had
I started my life with little to nothing
I've worked so hard
I've done so much
Now I'm thriving with my children by my side.

www.ingramcontent.com/pod-product-compliance
Lightning Source LLC
Chambersburg PA
CBHW051720130826
49812CB00034B/1274
9789357214438